THE LIFE & TIMES OF

Queen Elizabeth II

BY
Amy Dempsey

‖·PARRAGON·‖

This edition first published by
Parragon Book Service Ltd in 1996

Parragon Book Service Ltd
Unit 13–17 Avonbridge Trading Estate
Atlantic Road, Avonmouth
Bristol BS11 9QD

Produced by Magpie Books,
an imprint of Robinson Publishing

Illustrations courtesy of: Hulton Deutsch; Mirror
Syndication International; Peter Newark's Pictures

ISBN 0 75251 503 9

A copy of the British Library Cataloguing in Publication
Data is available from the British Library.

Typeset by Whitelaw & Palmer Ltd, Glasgow
Printed in Singapore

LILIBET, THE KING'S GRANDDAUGHTER

On Wednesday, 21 April 1926, at 2.40 a.m., the child who would become Queen Elizabeth II was born to Albert and Elizabeth, the Duke and Duchess of York, at 17 Bruton Street, the home of the Duchess's parents, Lord and Lady Strathmore. The birth was witnessed by the Secretary of State for Home Affairs, Sir William Joynson-Hicks, as was the custom, who then reported back to the Prime Minister, Stanley Baldwin, that only one child had been born, and that it had not been

The Duchess of York with her daughter, Elizabeth

swapped for another. The medical bulletin stated that 'a certain line of treatment' had been used, indicating a Caesarian section, and that mother and child were doing well. At Windsor Castle, King George V and Queen Mary were overjoyed when they were informed of the birth of their granddaughter.

By prophetic coincidence, the Queen's luncheon visitors that day were Princess Andrew of Greece and the Dowager Marchioness of Milford Haven, the mother and grandmother of the newborn's future husband. After lunch the King and Queen went to Bruton Street to congratulate 'Bertie' and Elizabeth, and to see the baby.

Although at the time of her birth, the new princess was third in line to the throne, there was very little expectation that she would ever reign, as her father was the second son of the King and Queen and his elder brother, Edward, Prince of Wales, England's most eligible bachelor, was the heir apparent. It was expected that he would shortly find a bride and produce his own line of succession. The pregnancy of the Duchess of York had been followed by the public, for Bertie and Elizabeth had been the country's most popular young couple since their wedding in April 1923. The baby's arrival was marked by a twenty-one gun salute at the Tower of London and in Hyde Park on the morning of 26 April.

On Saturday, 29 May, the princess was christened by the Archbishop of York in the private chapel of Buckingham Palace and baptized Elizabeth Alexandra Mary, with the King's approval. The six sponsors were the King, Queen and Lord Strathmore (grandparents), Princess Mary and Lady Elphinstone (aunts), and the Duke of Connaught, Queen Victoria's last surviving son.

As second in line to the throne, royal duties were a part of life for Bertie, and in January 1927 he and the Duchess set sail on a six-month tour of the Antipodes, to visit the Dominions and open the Australian Parliament in the new capital, Canberra. The baby princess stayed with her grandparents alternately, first with the Strathmores and then at Buckingham Palace with the King and Queen. The King became increasingly attached to the child, referring to her as 'sweet little Lilibet', the name she had given herself, in his journal and letters to her parents, prompting the Duke to write, 'I do hope you will not spoil her too much, as I have always been told grandfathers are apt to do.' On 27 June the Duke and Duchess returned from their successful tour and Princess Elizabeth, at fourteen months, made her first balcony appearance for the cheering crowds outside Buckingham Palace.

The Yorks now moved into their first home at 145 Piccadilly, which had been prepared for them while they were away. Lilibet's early days were spent between Piccadilly and the homes of her grandparents when her parents were called away on various royal duties. As much as was possible, the Duchess insisted upon a simple, normal, home life away from the glare of publicity, in an attempt to keep her daughter from becoming spoiled and spiteful.

In the autumn of 1928 King George became seriously ill with a lung infection and asked for Lilibet to be sent to him in Bognor during his convalescence. As he recovered he began to walk again, keeping one finger on his granddaughter's shoulder for balance, and an appearance on Easter Monday 1929 of the King, Queen, and tiny Princess at the sea wall in Bognor drew cheering crowds. Little Lilibet's popularity with the press and the public was soaring.

Elizabeth's love of horses began at an early age, with her nose pressed against the nursery window of 145 Piccadilly watching the horses go by, for horses were still in daily use in pre-war Britain. She had her first riding lessons in 1929, and for her fourth birthday in 1930 the King gave her a Shetland pony named Peggy. She loved going around the stables with her grandfather at Sandringham, the royal residence in Norfolk, and watching the village horses and ponies at Glamis Castle in Perthshire, her mother's family home.

Princess Margaret was born on 21 August

1930 when Lilibet was four years old. The two sisters quickly became fast friends and companions. Two years later King George V gave the Duke and Duchess of York the Royal Lodge at Windsor Great Park for their country home and the family spent many idyllic weekends there surrounded by pets and ponies. The people of Wales presented Little House, a miniature thatched house, to Elizabeth on her sixth birthday, so the girls had a house all of their own to care for and in which to entertain visitors.

Although her mother taught her to read, by the time Elizabeth was seven, the time had come for something slightly more structured. Marion Crawford, 'Crawfie', joined the household in 1933 as a live-in tutor and governess. A schoolroom was set up in the house at Piccadilly, and lessons, which later included Margaret, were started. As the chil-

The Royal Family, 1936

dren had been fairly successfully shielded from the public eye, Crawfie was able to take them out without their being recognized, for example, to Woolworths in Oxford Street for Christmas shopping. These trips were much preferable to the royal shopping trips to Harrods, and 'Grandpapa England' and 'Granny Queen's' collection soon included many china figurines from Woolworths to sit alongside their Fabergé treasures.

Public appearances usually resulted from family occasions, such as when Princess Elizabeth was a bridesmaid at the wedding of her uncle, Prince George, Duke of Kent, to Princess Marina of Greece in 1934, and again the following year when another uncle, Henry, Duke of Gloucester, married Lady Alice Scott. 1935 was also the year of the Silver Jubilee, celebrating twenty-five years of the reign of her grandfather, King George V.

Elizabeth and Margaret rode with their parents in the procession to St Paul's Cathedral, waving to the cheering crowds, and later appeared with the family on the balcony of Buckingham Palace to accept the public's adulation – two acts which they would both be doing innumerable times in the future.

Christmas 1935 saw the girls separated from their parents. The Duchess had severe flu and had to remain at Royal Lodge while the princesses went to Sandringham with Grandpapa King and Granny Queen. Christmas passed playing with relatives and in the snow with their new sleigh, listening to the broadcast of their grandfather's Christmas address to the nation, and waiting for their parents to arrive. But on 17 January, Queen Mary came to find them and told them that the King was very ill. Elizabeth was taken to his bedside to say her farewells and then the girls were sent to Royal Lodge. Three days later, at 11.55 p.m. on 20 January 1936, the King died.

At the King's death, Princess Elizabeth became second in line to the throne, as her uncle, David (as Edward, Prince of Wales was known), was still unmarried. Although the family was despairing of his liaison with Mrs Wallis Simpson (an American commoner, and a divorcee to boot), the third affair he had had with a married woman, no one really expected the new king to renounce his birthright and duty. That, however, was just what he did. On Thursday, 10 December 1936, after an eleven-month reign, King Edward VIII abdicated the throne, and the Duke of York became King George VI. It was left to Crawfie to attempt to explain the rapidly changing events, and their instant repercussions – having to curtsy to their parents, and the immediate move to Buckingham Palace. Neither were welcome changes, as the new King could not bear the symbolic barrier of his children curtsying to him, and it was ruled that such formality would only be required on formal public occasions. Likewise, upon hearing that they would have to live in Buckingham Palace, Lilibet, horrified, replied, 'You mean for ever?'

THE HEIRESS
PRESUMPTIVE

The Coronation that was to have been Edward VIII's became George VI's on 12 May 1937. Elizabeth and Margaret walked on either side of Princess Mary, the Princess Royal (the King's sister), and ahead of Queen Mary in the procession to Westminster Abbey. The day's events ended with more balcony appearances, and Lilibet wrote an account of the event as a gift for her parents, entitled 'To Mummy and Papa, in memory of their Coronation', which is stored in the Royal Archives at Windsor.

George VI's Coronation

While the new King and Queen settled into the duties of the roles they had never imagined having to fill, they also had to consider how to protect Elizabeth from the glare of attention that would fall on her as heiress presumptive, as well as how best to prepare her for the role that would now inevitably one day be hers – that of Queen. Lessons continued with Crawfie and a Girl Guide troop was formed at Buckingham Palace, which provided additional playmates. Interspersed amongst these daily activities were more adult, state, concerns, such as attending the State Opening of Parliament, participating in the State Visit of King Carol of Romania, and presenting the winning rosettes at the National Pony Show. Much to the relief of Crawfie, who was feeling the pressure of educating the heir to the throne, Lilibet was taken to Mr Henry Marten, the Vice-Provost of Eton, for private lessons in British constitutional history.

13

Elizabeth and Margaret were in Scotland at Balmoral when war broke out between Germany and Britain on 3 September 1939. Their parents returned to London and the family was reunited at Royal Lodge for Christmas. As the war escalated and the Nazi invasions in Europe continued, the girls were moved to Windsor Castle on 11 May 1940, where they would stay for the duration of the war. The King and Queen had decided not to send them to Canada, as some had advised, but their whereabouts was kept secret. Living quarters were set up in the massive dungeons of the castle, where other precious items were also stored, such as the Crown Jewels. Elizabeth's lessons with Mr Marten continued, focusing on an analysis of contemporary events.

Lilibet felt keenly that she should be doing more and in October 1940 finally convinced her father that she should make a broadcast to the children of the Empire, much as her mother had done earlier in the war to the women of France and Britain. In her first public broadcast, one can detect her beginning to see herself as a representative for her generation, speaking to fellow evacuees about the need to be strong and supportive during the difficulties of war. The broadcast was a success, and produced an avalanche of mail from children in Britain and overseas.

As the threat of invasion lifted somewhat, Lilibet was allowed to participate in activities with the outside world again. In 1942, just before her sixteenth birthday, she received her first military rank, being made Colonel-in-Chief of the Grenadier Guards. On her birthday she inspected her regiment in a march-past of 600 men, and gave a party for them afterwards. As she took to heart what she supposed her new duties to be – offering praise and criticism – perhaps a little too enthusiastically, a message reached her through her elders from one of the majors, 'You should perhaps tell the Princess quietly that the first requisite of a really good officer is to be able to temper justice with mercy.' This lesson, an important one for a future leader of any sort, was quickly learned.

Shortly after her sixteenth birthday Lilibet in Girl Guide uniform, went to the Labour Exchange in Windsor to register under the youth registration scheme of the National Service Act. While pestering her parents to be allowed to do more, like her older cousins who were already in the Women's Royal Naval Service (Wrens), Sir Alec Hardinge, the King's Private Secretary, sent her a newspaper clipping about her registration, reminding her that 'the Princess really became liable for National Service, of a very special kind, at her birth.'

Lilibet's involvement in the work of the 'family firm', as her father called it, increased as she turned eighteen. She became a Counsellor of State in July 1943 and attended her first official dinner in May 1944, seated between Field Marshal Jan Smuts of South Africa and William Mackenzie King of Canada at a dinner of the Dominion Prime Ministers at the Palace. Shortly afterwards, she was installed as President of the National Society for the Prevention of Cruelty to Children, giving her first presidential address. In August she undertook her first solo dress engagement, launching the battleship HMS *Vanguard*. All the while she had been insistent upon being allowed to join the ATS (Auxiliary Territorial Service), the women's service of the British Army. All eighteen-year-olds had to register for national service, and she did not want to be an exception. The King finally gave in and in March 1945 entry as Second Subaltern, ATS, was granted to No. 230873, Elizabeth Alexandra Mary Windsor. Age: eighteen. Eyes: blue. Hair: brown. Height: 5 foot 3 inches. She was sent to No. 1 Mechanical Transport Training Centre at Aldershot, where she learned basic mechanics and how to drive ambulances, buses and lorries. Her decision to join the ATS further endeared her to the public, and her instructor pronounced, 'Her Royal Highness is a very good and extremely considerate driver.'

As the war drew to its close, the public affection for the Royal Family escalated even more, for being there in the heart of the crises, for their strength and sense of duty to the nation. They became the focus for the celebrations on VE-Day, 8 May 1945. Winston Churchill, the Prime Minister, formally announced the end of the war against Germany, and the crowds outside Buckingham Palace went wild, chanting, 'We want the King!' The King and Queen, the Princesses, and Churchill appeared on the balcony to thunderous applause. The ovations did not let up and the family appeared on the balcony a total of eight times during the day. As night fell, with the masses of people still chanting and celebrating, Margaret and Elizabeth persuaded the King to let them join the crowds. He agreed, providing they wore headscarves and took escorts with them. They joined the celebrations, cheering every time the King and Queen appeared on the balcony, and then went dancing down the Mall with the revellers. According to Princess Margaret, 'It was absolutely wonderful. Everybody was knocking everybody else's hats off, so we knocked off a few, too. Everyone was absolutely marvellous. I never had such a beautiful evening.'

With peace (Japan surrendered in August 1945), one of the challenges for the King and Queen was how to prepare Elizabeth for her pending role as monarch by avoiding the pitfalls of past examples – priggishness and vanity from too much power at an early age, restlessness and idleness from too little, and boredom and frustration from being under the public microscope too much. They decided that she should have limited, controlled public exposure for as long as possible.

In early 1947 the King, Queen and Princesses set sail for South Africa, Elizabeth's first tour outside her home country. The aim of the visit was to pay tribute to South Africa's war effort and to try to quell the republicanism that threatened to take the Union out of the British Commonwealth. The family received a warm greeting despite the republicans, and the King opened the South African and Southern Rhodesian Parliaments. Elizabeth's twenty-first birthday was celebrated in South Africa with a parade, balls, and the declaration of a national holiday. The most important aspect of her 'coming out' was, however, Elizabeth's radio broadcast to the entire Commonwealth, in which she stated that 'I am 6,000 miles from the country where I was born, but I am certainly not 6,000 miles from home . . . I declare before you all that my whole life, whether it be long or short, shall be devoted to your service.' It was a declaration of intent to serve her people for as long as she is able.

Upon the family's return from South Africa in May, the next major issue was who was to be

Princess Elizabeth's 21st birthday broadcast

Elizabeth's partner in her service to the people of the Empire. Elizabeth considered the matter to be settled, for her romance with Prince Philip of Greece had begun long before the trip. She had wanted to become engaged before the tour, but the King and Queen had refused, in order to force the couple to consider long and hard, since there could be no change of heart. In addition to testing the couple's love, there were problems with Philip's lineage. He was a scion of the Greek monarchy, which had been imported to Greece from Denmark, and was of largely German descent. He also had, as one biographer put it, a number of 'inconvenient German relations', a problem in the immediate post-war period. When the Greek royal court was exiled by a revolutionary council in 1923, Philip was brought up by his mother's brothers in England, Lord Louis Mountbatten (later Earl Mountbatten of Burma) and

George, Marquess of Milford Haven. He had been educated at Cheam and Gordonstoun and then at the Royal Naval Academy, Dartmouth, and served in the Royal Navy during the war. It was this part of his past that was played up in the official accounts, and shortly after the war he renounced his Greek title, took his mother's maiden name of Mountbatten, and became a naturalized British citizen. With the clearing up of such details and the couple's obvious devotion to each other accepted, the engagement was formally announced on 10 July 1947. Philip was welcomed by the press and public, and *The Times* pronounced it 'a suitable match in every way'.

The date of the wedding was set for 20 November at Westminster Abbey. On the morning of the wedding, the King granted Philip the title of honour of 'His Royal

Elizabeth and Philip, an engagement photo

Highness', and conferred on him the titles Baron Greenwich, Earl of Merioneth, and Duke of Edinburgh, the latter being one of the Royal Family's titles last held by Queen Victoria's second son, Prince Alfred. The public's enthusiasm for the royal wedding was not shared by Clement Attlee's Labour government, however, which thought the extravagance inappropriate during such a time of austerity and rationing. Problems arose regarding the amounts to be paid the new couple from the Civil List, as a majority in the House of Commons they could see no reason for the Princess to be granted any further money, or her husband any at all. A compromise was eventually reached, granting Princess Elizabeth an allowance of £40,000 a year and Philip £10,000.

The wedding went beautifully and the couple honeymooned in Hampshire and the Highlands. Public reaction to the marriage was overwhelming and gifts streamed in from all over the world. For her part, the Princess followed through on her declaration to serve, on one occasion dividing up food parcels arriving from America and the Dominions to be sent overseas, and including a handwritten note with each one.

On 23 April 1948, six months after her wedding, Elizabeth was invested with the insignia of a Lady of the Most Noble Order of the Garter, on the 600th anniversary of the founding of the Order, the most ancient order of chivalry in the world. In rapid succession followed her twenty-second birthday and her parents' Silver Wedding anniversary. After these festivities, she and Philip went to France on their first major visit as a married couple. They were astounded and moved by their reception, on what proved to be the first of many successful visits to Paris.

Shortly after their return, the announcement was made that the Princess would 'undertake no public engagements after the end of June' as she was expecting her first child. On 14 November 1948, Prince Charles Philip Arthur George was born, just a few days after the first of three crucial operations was performed on his grandfather, King George VI. With the birth of Charles the family became impatient to move into Clarence House, which had been in the process of refurbishment since their wedding. On 4 July they moved into their new home, and almost immediately began to put their own stamp on the decoration by collecting contemporary paintings, mainly landscapes and seascapes, instead of borrowing works from the Royal Collection.

In October of 1949, Philip was posted to the destroyer HMS *Chequers* in the Mediterranean, and for the next eighteen months commuted between Malta and London, while Elizabeth did the same in reverse. The young couple enjoyed this time of travel and active careers, despite criticism about the effect it would have on their family, which expanded on 14 August 1950 with the arrival of Princess Anne Elizabeth Alice Louise. Their lifestyle was soon to be rapidly curtailed, however, though by another member of the family, the King. The illness of King George made it necessary for Elizabeth to deputize on his behalf at an ever-increasing number of events. By the summer of 1951 Philip had to take a leave of absence from the navy, to which he would never return to duty. Elizabeth presided as deputy during the State Visit of King Haakon of Norway and read her father's speech and acted for him at the Trooping the Colour during the King's Birthday Parade.

Meanwhile, a long-proposed trip by the Princess and the Duke of Edinburgh to tour Canada was to have seen them set sail on 25 September. But the King's health deteriorated, requiring an operation to remove his left lung, and the trip was put on hold. When the King appeared to be recovering the couple flew, after much deliberation by the Cabinet on their safety if they went by air, to Canada to be met by rapturous crowds. They crossed the continent twice, and made a side trip to Washington, DC, to visit President Harry Truman.

Upon their return the King appeared to have made good progress, though he still was not up to a proposed tour of Australia and New Zealand, and Elizabeth and Philip planned to go in his stead. On 30 January 1952 Elizabeth, Philip, Margaret and the King and Queen all went to the Drury Lane Theatre to see *South Pacific*, the last time they would all be together. The next morning, the King and Queen saw Elizabeth and Philip off at London Airport on the first part of their journey, to Nairobi. It was the last time Elizabeth would see her father. Within a week she would be Queen.

QUEEN ELIZABETH II

When Elizabeth learned of her father's death, she was on the banks of the Sagana River in the Aberdare Forest in Kenya. They had spent the morning at the observation post at Treetops, the famous hotel which then consisted of several log cabins built into a giant fig tree. Occasionally they had made excursions on the ground, at one point coming across a herd of forty-six elephants which appeared out of the bush near the Princess. Their host, Mr Jim Corbett, commented, 'Ma'am, if you have the same

courage in facing whatever the future sends
you as you have in facing an elephant at eight
paces, we are going to be very fortunate.'

The couple returned to Sagana Lodge for an
early lunch and at around 1.30 p.m. local
time on 6 February 1952, the Princess's
Private Secretary, Lieutenant-Colonel Martin
Charteris, was told by a local reporter that
the King was dead, although there was not
yet official confirmation. Nothing was said to
Elizabeth or Philip yet as Charteris tried to
confirm the report. He could not reach
anyone at Government House in Nairobi as
the Governor-General and his staff were *en
route* to Mombasa. Commander Michael
Parker, Prince Philip's Private Secretary, was
also on the case and from the tone of the
radio broadcasts presumed the news to be
true. He went around to the sitting-room of
the lodge, beckoned to Prince Philip from

the window, and told him the news. According to Parker, 'He looked as if you'd just dropped half the world on him,' which in essence was what had happened, for the Prince then had to break it to his wife that her beloved father had died and that she was now Queen. He took her along the river where they could have some privacy while the news sunk in.

While Prince Philip made plans for the return to England, matters of protocol had to be sorted out, for instance, the name Elizabeth would use as Queen. She could have used any of her Christian names, or any other, as her father's first name had been Albert but he had used his fourth name, George, upon accession. Charteris broached the subject, to which she answered, 'Oh, my own name, what else?' and began to write a series of telegrams postponing the rest of her trip to Australia and New Zealand signed 'Elizabeth R'.

It was arranged for a small plane to take them to Entebbe where they could board the *Argonaut Atlanta*, the plane that they had taken from London. The tiny airport was lined with local officials and townspeople paying their respects. The photographers were asked not to take any pictures of the Queen as her mourning clothes were to meet her at the *Argonaut*. After a three-hour delay in Entebbe, the flight finally took off around midnight with the Queen holding a radio message from her Prime Minister, Winston Churchill, which read, 'The Cabinet in all things awaits Your Majesty's command.'

Greeting their arrival in London on the afternoon of the 7th was a group of statesmen. The Queen's uncle, the Duke of Gloucester and Lord and Lady Mountbatten came on board the plane first to pay homage and offer their consolation. 'Shall I go down alone?' the Queen asked. 'I think you should,' Mountbatten replied. And so the Queen descended the steps alone to be received by her senior Privy Counsellors, Winston Churchill, Clement Attlee, Anthony Eden, Lord Woolton, Leader of the House of Lords, and Harry Crookshank, Leader of the House of Commons. Lord Woolton recalled, 'This symbolic scene . . . the new young Queen coming, unattended, down the gangway from her plane – was one that will never be forgotten . . .It was a period of deep emotion for everyone – and most certainly for the Queen, and yet, having shaken hands with each member of her Council, instead of going to her waiting car, she went along and spoke to the air crew – royal courtesy took precedence over private grief.'

The new Queen was greeted by the old Queen Mary upon her arrival at Clarence House. 'Her old Granny and subject,' Queen Mary had said, 'must be the first to kiss her hand.' Also waiting for her was the Duke of Norfolk, the Earl Marshal and Hereditary Marshal of England, whose duty it was to make the funeral arrangements for the late King. The following morning she met the Privy Council and made her Declaration of Sovereignty, and then returned to Clarence House to become the first monarch in history to watch her Proclamation on television.

The popular King was mourned and the new young Queen lauded. The King's brother, David, now Duke of Windsor, returned from semi-exile in France, for the funeral, but it was made known that his wife, Wallis, would not be welcome. He stayed with his mother at Marlborough House and after a meeting with the Queen and the Queen Mother realized that there was little hope of any lessening of the Royal Family's antagonism towards his wife. (His brother had allowed him the title of 'His Royal Highness', but denied it to his wife or descendants.)

The lying-in-state began on 11 February at Westminster Hall, and over 300,000 people filed by to pay their respects. The body was then taken by train to Windsor. The funeral ended with the Queen sprinkling the symbolic earth upon her father's coffin as it was lowered into the royal vaults at Windsor Castle.

Shortly after the funeral, Lord Mountbatten was overheard boasting that the House of Mountbatten now occupied the throne of Great Britain, Northern Ireland and the Dominions, as Elizabeth and Margaret were the last of the House of Windsor, and

Elizabeth was married to his nephew, now surnamed Mountbatten. Queen Mary was outraged and whipped Churchill and the Cabinet into a frenzy, which resulted in an official Order of Council on 21 April 1952 authorizing the Queen to retain her family name as the House of Windsor and for all her heirs to be so titled. The widowed Queen Consort also took this moment to call herself Queen Elizabeth the Queen Mother, a remarkable move as she technically ceased to have much in the way of a formal role upon the death of her husband and the succession of her daughter.

Now with the questions of names and titles settled, the question of residency arose again for Elizabeth. She and Philip were very fond of Clarence House and tried to convince Churchill that they should be allowed to continue living there. Churchill, however, believing that the monarch should have the principal palace as her official residence, refused, and for the second time in her life Elizabeth moved into Buckingham Palace against her desires.

In the next few months the Queen threw herself into the business of government and meeting all her ministers, and she carried out over 400 engagements in her first year, prompting a newspaper article from a doctor which suggested that measures should be taken in advance to ensure that 'Her Majesty's health and vitality will be protected from Her Majesty's hereditary sense of duty'.

The public's insatiable appetite for coverage of the Royal Family, which continues to this day, really began in Coronation Year, 1953. Elizabeth represented a link with the past and hope for a bright, new future. News of the 'fairytale princess' becoming Queen was a welcome diversion from the realities of post-war, recession–hit Britain. The events of 1953 – death, divorce, scandal, coronation, political crises – would provide many newspaper stories and lessons for the new monarch.

Queen Mary died at the age of eighty-six in March 1953, having left strict instructions in her will that the Coronation was to go on as planned. The Duke of Windsor again had to leave his wife behind while he attended his mother's funeral. The Coronation preparations were well under way, and included detailed rehearsals of the ceremony.

In the meantime, Princess Margaret had fallen in love with a distinguished ex-fighter pilot, Group Captain Peter Townsend, formerly an equerry to the late King, currently Comptroller of the Queen Mother's Household.

The problem was that he was divorced and Margaret was third in line to the throne. While the immediate family was sympathetic, the old guard in the Royal Household feared the repercussions of another scandal like that of the Duke of Windsor in 1936. Margaret, who needed her sister, the Queen's, permission to marry, was told that she should wait until her twenty-fifth birthday and then reapply.

The Coronation itself was filmed by the BBC and shown all over the world, and the street parties and other celebrations continued until well after midnight. What the television cameras failed to see, but an American reporter did not, was the obvious affection between Margaret and Townsend and speculation about another royal romance made foreign headlines. Two weeks later the *Sunday People* finally published the story in

The Coronation procession, 2 June 1953

Britain. Cries deploring a scandal were mixed with urgings that the couple should ignore protocol. Margaret left for Rhodesia with her mother, and Townsend was sent to be Air Attaché at the British Embassy in Brussels before her return.

The next problem for the Queen, though it was kept from the public, had a greater potential for disaster. On 23 June Winston Churchill suffered a stroke which, though serious, would not have provided a constitutional problem as such, except for the fact that his Foreign Secretary and Deputy Prime Minister, Anthony Eden, who would normally have taken over the direction of the government, was also critically ill. While Churchill's doctor, Lord Moran, put out a bulletin saying that the Prime Minister 'needed a rest', he secretly informed his confidants and family that Churchill's condition was severe. By the time his stroke was discovered, Churchill had recovered enough to deny its severity, to such an extent that very few people ever knew that for three months Britain had neither an acting Prime Minister nor a Foreign Secretary.

Churchill was fit enough to remain in office while, on 23 November 1953, the Queen embarked on her Commonwealth Coronation Tour, a six-month journey to demonstrate that 'the Crown is not merely an abstract symbol of our unity but a personal and living bond between you and me,' as the Queen stated in her Christmas address that year. The tour included Bermuda, Jamaica, Fiji, Tonga, New Zealand, Australia, Ceylon, Uganda, Malta, and Gibraltar, and was a fabulous public relations success. The Queen and Prince Philip returned to an elaborate homecoming in May of 1954.

In August 1955, Princess Margaret turned twenty-five and Fleet Street anxiously awaited the return of Townsend for the next chapter in the royal romance. The two years apart had not dampened their feelings for each other, and Margaret was under the impression that she would now be allowed to wed. Townsend returned in October, and the headlines became full of wild speculations. On 18 October, Anthony Eden, by then Prime Minister, joined the Royal Family at Balmoral and told the Queen that the marriage could not be approved by the Cabinet, and that if Margaret were to marry Townsend she would have to renounce her right to the throne, leave the country for a while, and lose her income from the Civil List. The position of the Queen as a symbol of moral and family values would be weakened if the marriage went ahead. In the end, Margaret sacrificed love for duty, and on 31

October 1955 issued a statement saying that she had decided not to marry Townsend. The couple went their separate ways, both later to marry; Townsend died in France, where he had lived for many years, in 1995.

During the remaining years of the 1950s, the Queen made State Visits to Norway, Nigeria, Sweden, Portugal, France, Denmark, Canada and the United States (twice), and the Netherlands, leading the American magazine, *Look*, to call her 'the most overworked young woman this side of the Iron Curtain'. The Duke of Edinburgh accompanied her on many of these trips while also making several excursions of his own, most notably a trip to the Antarctic. These absences were hard on Charles and Anne, and the number of times the couple were apart caused the press to speculate about marriage problems between their parents. These rumours were stayed somewhat when the Queen cancelled her tour of West Africa in 1959 due to pregnancy.

Also on the home front was the matter of Charles's schooling. He attended Hill House day school in Knightsbridge and then in 1958 was sent to Cheam, which fed into Gordonstoun, the public school at which his father had been educated. During his first term at Cheam, the Prince was hounded by the press to such an extent that the Queen, through her Press Secretary Commander Richard Colville, called a conference of newspaper editors to request that Charles be left alone or otherwise he would have to be taken out of the external educational system. The press cooled down for a while, but Charles was back in the headlines the next summer when his mother made him Prince of Wales.

It was in 1959, too, that the matter which had come to be known in the Cabinet as the 'Queen's Affair' was settled. While retaining the name of the Royal House, the Queen announced that her children and descendants were to bear the surname Mountbatten-Windsor, to which the Cabinet agreed. At the same Cabinet meeting, the wish of Princess Margaret to wed Antony Armstrong-Jones was put forward. Although a 'commoner' and one whose parents were divorced, the Cabinet agreed, and sent their best wishes and congratulations.

A royal tour to India, 1961

THE ROYAL FAMILY

Prince Andrew Albert Christian Edward was born on 19 February 1960, causing much excitement, since he was the first child born to a British Queen since Queen Victoria's last baby in 1857. The 1960s began a decade of family life for the Queen, with the birth of Prince Edward four years later. Two days after Andrew's birth Edwina, Countess Mountbatten died in Borneo, and two days after that Queen Victoria's last surviving grandson, Alexander, Marquis of Carisbrooke, died. A week of official court mourning was announced for the two deaths, and so too was the engagement of Princess Margaret to Mr Antony Armstrong-Jones. The palace was bombarded with cards of sympathy for the death and congratulations on the birth and engagement.

Princess Margaret's wedding took place in May in Westminster Abbey, Prince Philip giving away the bride before 300 million television viewers worldwide. For the time being, at least, Margaret finally seemed happy, and her first child was born on 3 November 1962, David Albert Charles. Tony Armstrong-Jones had just a month earlier finally accepted a title to become Earl of Snowdon, so that his heirs would be titled; his son was therefore given the courtesy title Viscount Linley. Before long, however, the Snowdons would be attracting a lot of negative publicity, both for their tempestuous relationship and for their extravagance.

The Queen's travelling continued, taking her to Cyprus, India, Pakistan, Nepal, Turkey, Italy, the Vatican, Ghana, Sierra Leone, the Gambia, Liberia, the Netherlands, New Zealand, Australia, and Fiji, until in October 1963 it was announced that she would undertake no further engagements pending the birth of her next child. Margaret, too, was pregnant, and the two sisters were joined for the holidays by two other expectant mothers, Princess Alexandra and the Duchess of Kent. Prince Edward Antony Richard Louis was born on 10 March 1964, followed by Margaret's daughter, Lady Sarah Frances Elizabeth Armstrong-Jones, on 1 May.

1965 was a year of family reconciliation and reunion. After the Queen's return from State Visits to Ethiopia and the Sudan, she was contacted by Lady Monckton, who had visited the Duke of Windsor while he was in

The Queen reviewing the Home Fleet,
River Clyde, 1965

hospital in London for an operation for a detached retina. Lady Monckton's message said that her uncle would be 'cheered and invigorated' by visits from his family. The Queen Mother's bitterness (she felt that the Duke's abdication had blighted her husband's life by thrusting him into the role of King) had subsided, and the Queen went to visit him on 15 March. The Duchess of Windsor was on hand for her first formal meeting with the Queen, having only met her once before when Elizabeth was ten years old. The Queen's visit signalled that tensions were easing, and other royal visitors called upon the Duke as a result.

In May of 1965 Elizabeth made a State Visit to Germany, which allowed her for the first time to visit the German relatives of both Philip and herself. It was the first visit by a British monarch to Germany since before the

Sandringham, 1969

First World War, and she received an ecstatic welcome from the Germans.

Next on the horizon was the question of Prince Charles's higher education. A small dinner party was given at Buckingham Palace by the Queen and Prince Philip to discuss the matter. The guests included the Prime Minister, Harold Wilson; Earl Mounbatten; the Archbishop of Canterbury, Dr Fisher; the Dean of Windsor, Dr Woods; Sir Charles Wilson, Chairman of the Committee of Vice-Chancellors; and Sir Michael Adeane, the Queen's Private Secretary. So many views were tabled that a committee was formed which finally recommended that the Prince should attend Trinity College, Cambridge, followed by a term in the Royal Navy.

The 1960s ended with two milestones. The Queen agreed to a proposal for a revolutionary television documentary, to be called *The Royal Family*. The film showed the members of the family in their personal and private lives, as well as at state functions and ceremonies. The BBC's first showing was a triumph, gripping 23 million viewers in Britain alone. One week later, Prince Charles was invested as Prince of Wales, only the second time the ceremony had occurred in 300 years of monarchy. The success of the documentary made this archaic pageantry seem less remote to the public, for Elizabeth and Charles were now seen by their subjects as mother and son, as well as symbols.

November 1972 marked the silver wedding anniversary of Philip and Elizabeth, and Prince Charles and Princess Anne planned a dinner party in their honour. In the afternoon, the family went for a walk through the streets of London, greeting the public and

The investiture of the Prince of Wales

receiving their best wishes. These 'walk-abouts' by the Queen were introduced in 1970 while on tour in New Zealand to coincide with a new down-to-earth image, more suited, it was thought, to monarchy in the late twentieth century.

The following May the engagement of Princess Anne and Captain Mark Phillips was announced, and they were married on Charles's birthday in November. The wedding received a great deal of coverage, much of it criticizing royal extravagance in the midst of a dire recession. There was something in this, for though the wedding was designated a family, rather than a state, occasion, which meant that the Queen paid the £140,000 bill for it, it had all the glittering adornments of a state affair.

On the 28 May 1973 the Duke of Windsor, once, briefly, King Edward VIII, died of can-

The Silver Jubilee, 1977

cer in Paris. His body was brought to England, and he was buried with all ceremony at Windsor. His widow, the former Mrs Simpson, and the cause of so much trouble for the House of Windsor, came from Paris for the service.

In the run-up to the Queen's Jubilee in 1977, celebrating twenty-five years of her reign, Princess Margaret was again the cause of scandal. Her marriage to Lord Snowdon was rapidly disintegrating and the press had carried photographs of her on holiday in Mustique with Roddy Llewellyn, who was thirteen years her junior, in January 1976. As the Townsend affair had blown up at the time of Elizabeth's Coronation, now twenty-five years later the scandal of Margaret's pending divorce occurred during the festivities surrounding her sister's reign. The announcement of the Snowdon's separation was made on 6 March, the same day on which Harold Wilson resigned as Prime Minister. The Queen's fiftieth birthday, on 20 April 1976, marked another outpouring of affection for her, however, which helped to detract from the problems caused by Margaret.

The Silver Jubilee included many tours – to Western Samoa, Fiji, Tonga, Papua New Guinea, Australia, New Zealand, Germany, Canada, Bahamas, Antigua, the British Virgin Islands and Barbados. Jubilee Day itself, 6 June, was a national holiday with street parties, torch processions and a re-enactment of the lighting of the beacons by Elizabeth I in 1588. There was a huge ceremonial procession led by the entire Royal Family through London to St Paul's, followed by a walkabout to the Guildhall. The week of events in London culminated in a thirty-minute fireworks display on the Thames. The events of year were rounded off nicely with Princess Anne announcing that she was expecting the Queen's first grandchild, and with Prince Charles making his own tours of Africa and Canada.

FAMILY TRIALS

While the Queen's popularity was at an all time high, Princess Margaret's continued to decline. Her affair with Llewellyn continued, she was hospitalized for alcoholic hepatitis, and her divorce was announced in May, all prompting suggestions that she should retire from public life. Pressure grew until Llewellyn accepted voluntary banishment abroad as had Townsend decades before. Another tragedy befell the family when Lord Mountbatten was killed by an IRA bomb in Ireland in 1979. The Queen and Prince Charles led the mourning,

The Queen and Commonwealth Prime Ministers, 1977

she having lost one of her staunchest supporters and he having lost his favourite great-uncle, confidant and adviser.

The 1980s brought a renewed increase in travelling by the Queen, but this time as an ambassador for British trade and industry. Media interest in the monarchy subsided for a while, only to be unleashed with new vigour in the coming years. In 1980 Prince Charles was thirty-two years old and bought himself a family home, Highgrove in Gloucestershire, which led to speculation that he was ready to marry and settle down after a long string of girlfriends. Charles met the nineteen-year-old Lady Diana Spencer that summer. Within the space of a few months, Diana went from being the younger sister of one of Charles's previous girlfriends to becoming his fiancée.

After the formalities of seeking his mother's

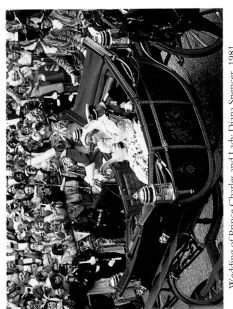

Wedding of Prince Charles and Lady Diana Spencer, 1981

approval and that of the Privy Council, they became engaged on 24 February 1981. Diana-mania was unleashed, and interest in the British monarchy was restored, albeit to an hysterical level. Prince Charles had found a fairytale princess to continue in the line of his mother. Britain of the early 1980s, with increased IRA terrorist activity, the deepening recession, rioting in Brixton and Toxteth, and the Prime Minister, Mrs Thatcher's 'experiments', needed the diversion of a royal wedding.

The wedding itself, which was held on 29 July 1981 at St Paul's Cathedral instead of Westminster Abbey, drew unprecedented media interest, both at home and abroad. The media coverage did not abate after the wedding, and early in 1982 a meeting of all the Fleet Street editors had to be called at Buckingham Palace to try to strike a balance in the coverage, and so ease the stress on the Princess, who was by then pregnant.

Also in 1982, Britain went to war with Argentina over the Falkland Islands, during which the twenty-two-year-old Prince Andrew served as a helicopter pilot. As such, the Queen's involvement was not only as a monarch and titular Commander-in-Chief of the British forces, but as a mother. On 21 June, one week after the liberation of the Falklands on the 14th, Prince William Arthur Philip Louis was born to the Prince and Princess of Wales, giving further cause for celebration.

In July Michael Fagan, an unemployed labourer, broke into Buckingham Palace, finding his way to the Queen's bedroom where he claimed he was going to slash his wrists. He sat talking to the Queen for some minutes until she was able to summon help, which was very slow in arriving. This incident, which turned out to be Fagan's second break-in at the Palace, coupled with the long response time of the police, raised grave questions about the security system at the Palace. Shortly afterwards, the Queen had to dismiss her personal bodyguard, Commander Michael Trestrail, who was being blackmailed by a male prostitute. Later, in July, two IRA bomb attacks in Hyde Park and Regent's Park killed eleven of the Queen's soldiers and seven of their horses. These events clearly shook the Queen and she was ordered to rest. She began to cheer up, however, when Anne returned from a tour of America and Andrew from service in the Falklands.

Press coverage in the 1980s concentrated on Diana's fashions, Prince Andrew's latest girlfriends, and the disharmony between

Anne and Mark, and a number of former employees of the Royal Family sold stories and photographs to the tabloids. Another woman grabbing headlines at this time was the Prime Minister, Margaret Thatcher, whom the Queen saw less than eye to eye with on many issues, particularly her government's policies at home, which the Queen regarded as 'uncaring and socially divisive'. The tensions between the two were kept well hidden, for the Queen stuck to the belief that she was constitutionally bound to keep her private thoughts on political matters to herself, and that the monarch should be an apolitical, impartial referee. But these tensions came to a head in 1986 when Thatcher refused to invoke economic sanctions against South Africa, as the rest of the Commonwealth members insisted, and an article appeared in the *Sunday Times* which said that the Queen was 'dismayed' by Mrs Thatcher's policies both abroad and at home. The Palace issued a statement that it was preposterous that the Queen would have sanctioned the article, as she took her constitutional role very seriously. The statement also made it clear, however, that the Queen sees her role in the governance of the country as a very active one, giving her opinions clearly to the government, albeit confidentially.

On 19 March 1986 the Queen announced the engagement of Prince Andrew to Miss Sarah Ferguson, and a new royal star was born. Shortly afterwards was the Queen's sixtieth birthday, which was followed, on 24 April, by the death of the Duchess of Windsor at her home in Paris, aged eighty-nine. Her coffin was flown to England and she was buried at Windsor beside her husband.

Prince Andrew was granted the title Duke of

The Queen and Prince Philip, Ascot, 1986

York, and married Sarah Ferguson in an extravagant display of pageantry on 23 July. Sarah, whom the tabloid newspapers dubbed 'fun-loving Fergie', soon fell foul of the press and quickly took the place previously held by Princess Margaret and Princess Anne as the object of ridicule and criticism.

It was in 1986, too, that the Queen made a visit to China, during which she was followed by more than 200 Western journalists. Prince Philip stole the headlines this time, being dubbed the 'Great Wally of China' after being overheard remarking that if he stayed there much longer he would end up with slitty eyes, and that the Forbidden City was 'ghastly'.

By 1987 news coverage of the expanded Royal Family had spiralled totally out of control, with scarcely a day going by without a 'royal' headline, to the point at which Joe Haines, former press secretary to Harold Wilson, remarked that the Royal Family had become 'The Westenders', the only worldwide soap opera in existence. He laid the blame on both the family and the newspapers, and called for a break in the coverage. No break was forthcoming, and the press began to carry suggestions that the Queen should exercise more control over her family's activities. Unlike Princess Anne, who had taken on board her mother's sense of duty and threw herself into international charitable work, the three princes seemed to be floundering. Prince Charles, nearing forty, needed something more substantial to do; Prince Andrew had made an unsuccessful entry into the family business of public engagements until giving up and returning to naval duty; and the naive Prince Edward was recovering from the shock that an interview he had given, in which he had explained his change of career from the Royal Marines to show business, had received such widespread coverage. Prince Philip, too, took a battering, with criticism about his bullying child-rearing techniques and his lack of compassion or warmth, particularly to his sons. Unfortunately, the worst was yet to come.

1987 continued with increasing speculation about the health of Charles and Diana's marriage, and then the spotlight was turned on Princess Anne in Paris and her friendship with the actor Anthony Andrews. The pregnancy in 1988 of the Duchess of York provided a diversion, and drew an unheard-of amount of coverage. The birth of the Yorks' first child, Princess Beatrice, on 8 August that year commanded as much attention as had the assassination of President John F. Kennedy.

Princess Anne's marriage had effectively been

over for a number of years, and she had been pleading with the Queen to be allowed to end it. A box of letters to her from Commander Timothy Lawrence, the Queen's equerry, was stolen and sent to the *Sun*. It was hinted that this was a major cause of the breakdown of the marriage, but there was also the as-yet unpublished allegation that Mark Phillips had fathered a daughter by Heather Tonkin in New Zealand. The separation of Anne and Mark was announced in August 1989. For a cash payment, Phillips renounced all claims to his wife's or the Queen's property, did not contest Anne's custody of the children, and signed a bond of confidentiality.

The Queen's wealth became a major topic of controversy in 1990. Being exempt from paying income tax or death duties and receiving a Civil List allowance for herself and key family members, the House of Windsor fortunes were rapidly increasing. At the end of 1990 *Harper's & Queen* listed her as the world's wealthiest woman. This was an issue that had been brought up many times before, most notably in the 1970s when an attempt was made to distinguish between what was considered the Queen's personal property as opposed to national property. The Queen was still opposed to paying income tax, although Prince Charles voluntarily did (and does) so.

The 'fairytale' marriages of the Queen's three eldest children continued to disintegrate very publicly. 1992 was indeed to be an '*annus horribilis*', as Elizabeth was to call it in a speech at a dinner in the Guildhall in the City of London. On 19 March, exactly six years after their engagement, the separation of Prince Andrew and the Duchess of York was announced. This was followed in June by the publication of Andrew Morton's best-selling book, *Diana, Her True Story*, which chronicled the Princess of Wales's depression, bulimia, suicide attempts and problems with Charles. The ensuing publicity prompted the first discussion between Charles and his mother about the rumours of the breakdown of his marriage, during which he confirmed her worst fears – namely, that the marriage was indeed in trouble, that it had been a marriage of duty, and that both he and Diana had had enough. The rest of the summer proved just as despairing. Princess Anne and Mark Phillips's divorce was finalized, and then new scandal erupted in August. Photographs of a topless Duchess of York with her 'financial adviser' John Bryan, in the South of France hit the papers, followed four days later by the 'Squidgy' tapes – the transcript of an intimate telephone conversation between the Princess of Wales and James Gilbey, dating from New Year's Eve 1989. The year continued its downward spiral with the announcement of the separation of the Prince and Princess of Wales on 9 December, the Queen finally agreeing to pay income tax, and the fire at Windsor Castle, which did severe damage.

But 1993 started no better. As the New Year began, Princess Margaret was hospitalized for pneumonia, and began to complain bitterly how much happier her life would have been had she been allowed to marry Peter Townsend forty years earlier, her bitterness seemingly renewed by all the royal divorces pending around her. The next bomb to drop occurred on 'Black Wednesday', 13 January 1993, with the publishing of the transcripts of telephone calls containing 'dirty talk' between Prince Charles and Camilla Parker Bowles, Charles's long-time mistress and the wife of

Talking with local children at Sandringham, Christmas 1993

his friend, Brigadier Andrew Parker Bowles of the Household Cavalry. This was particularly devastating for the Queen, since it concerned her son and heir and thus threatened the very fabric of the monarchy. Then, in April, Andrew finalized his financial settlement with Sarah, which effectively ended the marriage.

It was a particularly harrowing time, and would have been for any family – the Queen's sister and three children all divorced or in the process of painful and very public separations, compounded by the fact that the Royal Family is an institution which cannot accept divorce, and that, for its members, the disgrace of 'Edward and Mrs Simpson' is always a shadow in the background.

A time of healing and rebuilding was necessary for the Queen and her family, both for the survival of the monarchy and the futures of her children. Over the next two years, both Charles and Diana began to regain their self-respect and dignity through their individual public engagements and charitable works, though they have since both made public statements admitting adultery, and tending to cast blame upon each other. Andrew and Sarah worked out a civilized relationship with each other, and Prince Edward, who suffered from accusations of homosexuality, began to date various beautiful young women.

The VE-Day and VJ-Day celebrations in May and August of 1995 brought an unexpected surge of affection for the Royal Family as enormous crowds gathered around Buckingham Palace for a glimpse of the family which had suffered so much, and especially for the Queen and the Queen Mother, who had stood on the same balcony fifty years earlier. Having sur-

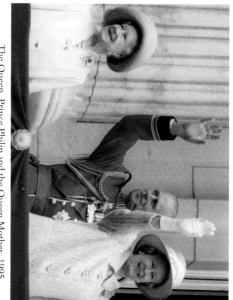

The Queen, Prince Philip and the Queen Mother, 1995

vived the Abdication, and thus the unexpected sovereignty of George VI, the war, and innumerable family blunders and scandals, these two women have earned the respect and affection of millions, even amongst those who would like to abolish the monarchy, as having genuinely done their best to serve and uphold the ideals of that monarchy.

As Queen Elizabeth II approaches her seventieth birthday, which falls on 21 April 1996, the future of the monarchy is far from assured. But one thing is certain: that she will continue to do that which she declared on her twenty-first birthday – to serve her people all her life.